Who Were The Brothers Grimm?

Who Were The Brothers Grimm?

By Avery Reed
Illustrated by John O'Brien

Grosset & Dunlap
An Imprint of Penguin Random House

For Derek, my first reader and love—AR

GROSSET & DUNLAP
Penguin Young Readers Group
An Imprint of Penguin Random House LLC

Published by Grosset & Dunlap, an imprint of Penguin Random House LLC, 345 Hudson Street, New York, New York 10014. GROSSET & DUNLAP is a trademark of Penguin Random House LLC. Printed in the USA.

Library of Congress Cataloging-in-Publication Data is available.

ISBN 978-0-448-48314-6 10 9 8 7 6 5 4 3 2 1

Contents

Who Were The Brothers Grimm?

"Once upon a time," an old peasant woman began, "there was a queen whose husband had been dead for many years, and she had a beautiful daughter."

A young man named Wilhelm Grimm listened attentively to the woman's story. The woman had likely heard it when she was a young child from her own mother.

It was a German fairy tale called "The Goose Girl." The fairy tale is about a magical charm, a horse who can speak, an evil servant, and a princess who seems doomed to a life guarding geese for a king who believes she is a peasant.

Wilhelm had traveled out into the countryside of Germany to meet Dorothea Viehmann and listen to her stories. She told him thirty-five tales—and Wilhelm wrote them all down, word for word.

It was 1813, and Wilhelm and his older brother, Jacob, were in the middle of a big project. The brothers had just published their first book together, a collection of German fairy tales, and now they were working on a second volume.

Jacob and Wilhelm Grimm were serious scholars, but they loved listening to fairy tales. They thought children's stories were an important part of German history. Because fairy

tales had been told and retold for hundreds of years, the tales showed how German language and culture had developed. But by 1813, fewer and fewer people were telling fairy tales to their children. Soon, the Grimms feared, no one would remember the stories.

It was difficult for Jacob and Wilhelm to collect fairy tales because the stories were not in books. Before the Grimms, very few fairy tales had ever been written down. People only came to know a fairy tale because someone else had told it to them. The only way to collect the stories was to listen to storytellers, like Dorothea, who knew them by heart.

What makes a story a fairy tale? A fairy tale is a quest story that is almost always about a very lucky hero who overcomes evil. A fairy tale also usually involves magic. There are imaginary creatures, such as fairies, giants, dragons, and elves. Sometimes there are even talking animals.

A fairy tale is set a long time ago in a faraway place, and usually begins with the phrase "once upon a time."

No one knows who first created fairy tales. These stories have simply developed over time. Sometimes, storytellers changed the stories slightly and added details as they went. Different versions of the same stories developed in different countries. In Germany, Snow White lived with seven dwarves. But in Albania, she lived with forty dragons.

Mothers and nursemaids told fairy tales like "Snow White" to children while cooking dinner, sitting by the fire, or before going to bed. Men and women also told these stories to one another while they worked, spinning wool or tending to their flocks.

As Wilhelm listened to Dorothea's stories, he never imagined that he and his brother would become famous. All he knew was that they wanted to write down these tales. Wilhelm wanted new generations of children to know and love Cinderella, Sleeping Beauty, Tom Thumb, and Little Red Riding Hood as much as he did.

Chapter 1
Best Friends

Jacob Ludwig Carl Grimm was born on January 4, 1785. Just thirteen months later, on February 24, 1786, his brother, Wilhelm Carl Grimm, was born. The boys' parents, Philipp and Dorothea Grimm, were thrilled.

At that time, there was no country called Germany—just a lot of German-speaking states that were part of the Holy Roman Empire. The Grimm family lived in a small town in the state of Hesse-Kassel.

Philipp Grimm worked as a lawyer and served as the town's clerk. Dorothea ran the household.

She had four more children: Carl, Ferdinand, Ludwig, and Charlotte, who was called Lotte. Two housemaids, Gretchen and Marie, helped Dorothea cook and care for the children. Sometimes, Gretchen would sneak the boys bread and cheese, and tell them fairy tales.

From an early age, Jacob and Wilhelm were inseparable. They slept together in one bed and studied at one desk. They pretended to hunt turkeys and spied on neighbors from their father's study window.

THE HOLY ROMAN EMPIRE

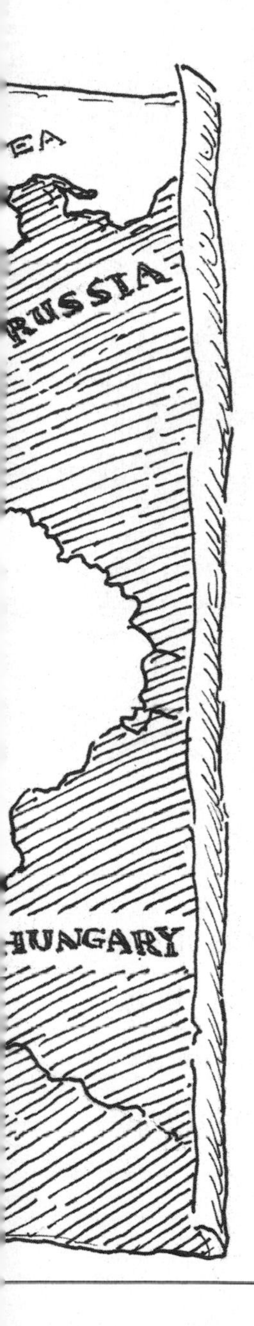

FROM 800 TO 1806, HUNDREDS OF CITIES AND STATES IN EUROPE WERE JOINED TOGETHER IN WHAT WAS CALLED THE HOLY ROMAN EMPIRE. THE EMPIRE WAS A CONFUSING PATCHWORK OF STATES THAT DIFFERED IN SIZE AND POWER. SOME WERE NO BIGGER THAN A SINGLE TOWN. THE LARGEST PART OF THE HOLY ROMAN EMPIRE WAS THE KINGDOM OF GERMANY.

BY THE TIME THE GRIMMS WERE BORN, THERE WERE 360 DISTINCT STATES. SOME WERE RULED BY KINGS AND PRINCES, OTHERS WERE RULED BY COUNTS AND LORDS. THE DIFFERENT RULERS WERE OFTEN POWER HUNGRY AND WENT TO WAR AGAINST ONE ANOTHER. BECAUSE OF THIS, THE HOLY ROMAN EMPIRE WAS NOT A STRONG EMPIRE. IN 1806, NAPOLEON BONAPARTE, THE EMPEROR OF FRANCE, FORCED THE GERMAN EMPEROR FRANCIS II TO DISSOLVE IT.

Jacob was small and slender, but he was strong willed and determined. Wilhelm was taller than Jacob and much more sensitive. He loved poetry and art. Both boys were smart and hardworking.

Though they were bright and curious, Jacob and Wilhelm hated school. Jacob, who had read full newspaper articles from age five, found their lessons very boring. Their teacher, Herr Zinckhan, was also mean. If a student forgot his grammar book, Zinckhan would give him a beating.

The Grimm family was very close. Jacob and Wilhelm helped take care of their younger siblings. Their aunt Julianne taught the brothers to read and write. Their parents taught the children to be proud they were German and to trust in God in difficult times.

In 1791, when Jacob was six and Wilhelm was five, their father became the magistrate, or judge, in a nearby town. The Grimm family moved into a beautiful home with a huge lime tree out front.

By 1792, war had broken out in France, and the countries surrounding France were pulled into the conflict. French soldiers wandered the streets near the Grimms' home. Dorothea did not allow Jacob and Wilhelm outdoors when the soldiers were near. The townspeople complained that the soldiers were disorderly. This made Philipp's job difficult, and he was often away from his family.

Still, he was very active in the boys' lives, praying with them in the morning and asking them questions at dinner. Jacob and Wilhelm were very proud of their father, especially when he was wearing his judge's uniform.

Then, on January 10, 1796, six days after Jacob's eleventh birthday, their father died suddenly. The Grimm family was devastated.

Besides being so sad, they now had very little money. Dorothea could not work and raise six children on her own. One of the boys' aunts helped Dorothea around the house. She also arranged for Jacob and Wilhelm to study at a school near her home in the city of Kassel.

The boys were sad to leave their mother and siblings. But Dorothea insisted they go. This was their one chance for a good education.

Chapter 2
A Proper Education

Jacob started school right away, but Wilhelm had to be privately tutored for a year before he was ready. At their new school, the brothers felt like outsiders. They were far behind the other students, most of whom were children of noblemen. The boys' classmates made fun of them, and their teachers were not much kinder. But Jacob and Wilhelm worked hard. Each morning before school, they spent four hours being tutored in Latin and French. They also studied geography, natural history, and other subjects for six hours each day.

Soon, their hard work paid off. Jacob, especially, excelled at his studies. By the time he graduated, he was first in his class!

UNIVERSITY OF MARBURG

In the spring of 1802, Jacob was accepted at the university at Marburg. For the first time in their lives, the brothers would live apart.

Marburg was a beautiful city built directly into the side of a steep hill. At the very top of the hill sat a castle. The university was just below.

Jacob decided to study law, as his father had, but he wasn't very interested in the subject. He later said that he should have chosen botany, the study of plants. Jacob spent hours wandering the hillsides around Marburg, sketching and admiring the flowers and trees.

In the fall of 1803, Wilhelm joined Jacob in Marburg. He decided to study law, too. Both thought they would end up as judges, like their father.

But the brothers' love for literature was growing. While their classmates spent their free time drinking beer and gambling, Jacob and Wilhelm discussed books and dance, and sometimes acted out plays.

One of their favorites was Shakespeare's *A Midsummer Night's Dream*. They even dressed in costumes. The brothers also loved to tell each other children's stories: myths, fables, and fairy tales. They were much poorer than their classmates. However, Wilhelm and Jacob only seriously complained when they didn't have enough money to buy books.

AESOP'S FABLES

AESOP (620 BC–564 BC) WAS AN ANCIENT GREEK STORYTELLER WHO IS CREDITED WITH WRITING MANY TALES, NOW KNOWN AS *AESOP'S FABLES*. A FABLE IS A STORY THAT ALWAYS HAS A MORAL—OR A LESSON—AT THE END. THE CHARACTERS ARE OFTEN TALKING ANIMALS. "THE TORTOISE AND THE HARE" IS ABOUT A TURTLE THAT WALKS VERY SLOWLY BUT STILL WINS A RACE AGAINST A SPEEDY RABBIT. THIS STORY SHOWS THAT TAKING YOUR TIME IS BETTER THAN DOING SOMETHING QUICKLY. THE PHRASE "SLOW AND STEADY WINS THE RACE" COMES FROM THIS FABLE.

ALTHOUGH SOME PEOPLE DOUBT THAT A WRITER NAMED AESOP EVER ACTUALLY EXISTED, THIS COLLECTION OF STORIES HAS SURVIVED AND REMAINED POPULAR FOR WELL OVER A THOUSAND YEARS! *AESOP'S FABLES* IS STILL THE MOST POPULAR BOOK OF FABLES IN THE WORLD. SOME OF THE MOST FAMOUS ARE "THE BOY WHO CRIED WOLF," "THE GOOSE THAT LAID THE GOLDEN EGGS," "THE LION AND THE MOUSE," AND "THE FOX AND THE GRAPES."

Chapter 3
A New Idea

Jacob suggested that Wilhelm take a class from his favorite professor, Friedrich Karl von Savigny. Most professors talked and talked, and expected students to write down everything without asking any questions. Professor Savigny, however, encouraged questions from his students and asked many of his own.

Professor Savigny thought Jacob and Wilhelm were smart and talented. He noticed that they enjoyed discussing many of the same topics that he did. So he invited them to his house to meet other writers and thinkers.

One evening, Jacob walked into Professor Savigny's library. Every wall was covered with books. Jacob was amazed! He couldn't stop looking at all of them. His eyes landed on a volume of German songs from the Middle Ages. He took it off the shelf and began to read. He could barely understand it. The songs were written in an older version of German.

It was different from the German that Jacob spoke. Still, he was fascinated by songs that emphasized German pride, culture, and history.

Jacob and Wilhelm spent many evenings at Professor Savigny's home. He taught them how to study old manuscripts, and to pay close attention to the details that made these historical books important.

At that time, many professors taught that the history of ancient Greece and Rome was more important than German history, literature, and ideas. But Savigny disagreed, and so did the Grimms.

At Savigny's house, Jacob and Wilhelm met many writers and artists who also cared about German history. One was a poet named Clemens Brentano.

CLEMENS BRENTANO

He was a loud, lively man who was brimming with ideas for new projects.

One of his ideas was to collect German folk songs. Folk songs are old songs that people have sung for generations. Like fairy tales,

they were rarely written down. Brentano was afraid the songs were going to be forgotten. So he and another writer, Achim von Arnim, began collecting the words to old folk songs. They wanted to publish them as a book.

Jacob and Wilhelm loved this idea. They were quickly becoming more interested in German literature than German law.

In 1804, Savigny moved to Paris, France. A year later, he asked Jacob to join him and work as his assistant. With permission from his mother, Jacob dropped out of the university and set off for Paris. Savigny was studying ancient Roman law. He asked Jacob to read many different versions of the same book to see which one was most accurate. Many people would find this job very boring, but Jacob loved it. Jacob loved Paris, too. He wrote Wilhelm many letters describing the people, the food, and even the buildings. It was the first time Jacob saw a world beyond the small towns of Germany.

Brentano and Arnim's collection of German folk songs was published the same year Jacob moved to Paris. It was called *The Boy's Magic Horn*. The authors included an introduction that challenged all German writers to copy down and preserve as many folk songs as possible.

The book certainly had not included them all! And Arnim and Brentano did not want any folk songs to be lost.

The Grimms decided to take up the challenge. Although they lived apart, Jacob and Wilhelm wrote letters back and forth asking if the other had discovered any new stories or songs for children. The brothers were very interested in starting their own collection.

Chapter 4
A Grimm Time

After living in Paris for ten months, Jacob returned to Kassel, where Wilhelm, their mother, and their siblings were living. Wilhelm studied for his final exams at the university, and Jacob found a job as a clerk at the state's war office.

War was coming. Napoleon Bonaparte was the emperor of France. It was 1805, and Napoleon had taken control of Italy, Austria, Egypt, and Turkey. Now he was coming for Germany.

NAPOLEON BONAPARTE

TYPES OF STORIES

THERE ARE MANY DIFFERENT TYPES OF STORIES THAT THE GRIMMS WOULD HAVE HEARD AS CHILDREN.

A **FOLKTALE** IS A STORY OF THE COMMON PEOPLE: FISHERMEN, FARMERS, SHEPHERDS, AND PEASANTS. FOLKTALES DEVELOPED AS PEOPLE TOLD STORIES TO ONE ANOTHER WHILE THEY WORKED OR COMPLETED HOUSEHOLD TASKS.

A **FAIRY TALE** IS A STORY THAT TELLS HOW A LUCKY HERO OVERCOMES EVIL. THE STORY IS NOT SET IN ANY PARTICULAR TIME OR PLACE AND

ALWAYS INCLUDES MAGIC. FAIRY TALES SOMETIMES FEATURE TALKING ANIMALS, FAIRIES, AND OTHER IMAGINARY CREATURES. THERE ARE OFTEN REPETITIONS OF THREE OR SEVEN, SUCH AS THREE BROTHERS, THREE WISHES, OR SEVEN DWARVES. FAIRY TALES ALMOST ALWAYS BEGIN WITH THE PHRASE "ONCE UPON A TIME."

A **LEGEND** IS A TRADITIONAL STORY ABOUT A REAL PLACE, TIME, OR PERSON. MUCH OF THE STORY IS MADE UP, BUT THE STORY IS BASED LOOSELY ON HISTORY. KING ARTHUR WAS A REAL BRITISH KING, BUT HE DID NOT ACTUALLY PULL A SWORD OUT OF A STONE. THAT IS A LEGEND.

A **FABLE** IS A SHORT STORY THAT IS MEANT TO TEACH A LESSON. TALKING ANIMALS ARE TYPICALLY THE MAIN CHARACTERS IN THE STORIES.

On November 1, 1806, French soldiers seized Kassel, and the German noblemen fled. The brothers' aunt, who had brought them to Kassel for school, left too.

Almost overnight, the entire town changed. French, not German, was now the language spoken in Kassel. Life became very difficult for Jacob and Wilhelm. Their home was occupied by foreigners, and their favorite aunt no longer lived nearby. The brothers felt very alone. Jacob quit his job, and Wilhelm could not find work. To take their minds off all their troubles, Jacob and Wilhelm concentrated more and more on collecting German fairy tales. They scoured libraries and bookshops for fairy tales. But they had little luck finding any.

Then, in May 1808, Dorothea Grimm suddenly died. She had been the center of family life: It was her love and support that had created such a close and happy home. The brothers had lost their jobs. Now they had lost their mother, too! This was the most difficult time for the Grimm family.

Lotte ironed clothes. Neighbors shared their food, and Jacob and Wilhelm helped with the housework. Still, they only ate one meal a day.

Things began to improve when their younger brother Ludwig found work. He became an illustrator for a literary journal that Arnim and Brentano edited. Then, in July, King Jerome,

Napoleon's brother who now ruled Kassel, hired Jacob to run the palace library. There were twelve thousand books in the library. However, no one but the king, queen, and librarian were allowed to read them. That wasn't fair. Still, it was the perfect job for Jacob. He spent his days reading and studying—and he was paid to do it!

Wilhelm was in poor health and seemed to get worse each day. He would lose his breath after climbing a few steps. His heartbeat was very irregular. It would beat very quickly before returning to normal. Sometimes this would continue for almost a whole day! Getting good care was hard. In 1809, Wilhelm traveled sixty miles to see a doctor in Halle.

When he wasn't being treated or resting, Wilhelm looked through all the books in the library in Halle for fairy tales. Wilhelm found some folk songs but very few fairy tales. The brothers' collection was off to a slow start.

Finally, after six months, Wilhelm began to feel better, so much so that he accepted Arnim's invitation to visit him in Berlin. There, Arnim introduced him to many writers and artists,

who inspired Wilhelm to contribute to the world beyond his small hometown. This trip was to Wilhelm what Paris had been to Jacob. It opened his eyes to the larger world. In December 1809, Wilhelm returned home to Kassel.

With French secret police roaming the city, Jacob and Wilhelm retreated to their study. They studied German history and literature that was written hundreds of years earlier. Many of the books they wanted to read were in old and foreign languages. But Jacob and Wilhelm were not bothered by this. They simply taught themselves to read over ten languages, both ancient and modern. And they did all of this without language guides or textbooks!

Of all the literature they read, Jacob and Wilhelm loved reading fairy tales the best. Many smart people thought fairy tales were simple and childish. The Grimms, however, believed that fairy tales were hidden treasures of German culture and values.

The brothers wanted to remind people what it meant to be German, even while under French rule and especially during a time of war. They thought saving German fairy tales was the way to do it. But if fairy tales weren't in bookstores and libraries, where could the brothers find them?

Chapter 5
Collecting Fairy Tales

One day, Arnim sent Jacob and Wilhelm two fairy tales. A storyteller had told these stories by heart, from memory. "The Juniper Tree" was the story of an evil stepmother who kills her stepson. "The Fisherman and His Wife" was the story of a poor fisherman and his greedy wife who is never satisfied with the gifts they receive from a magical fish.

Up until this point, Jacob and Wilhelm had been trying to find fairy tales in books. Now they had two authentic German fairy tales directly from a *storyteller*! Jacob and Wilhelm decided to look for other storytellers and write down their tales exactly as they told them.

Before people used writing to record information, they handed down their history, beliefs, and way of life by telling stories. Fairy tales were important. Not only did they provide entertainment, they also taught children about growing up. Fairy tales were about facing challenges and overcoming them.

No matter how big a giant might be or how scary a dragon is, the hero is always able to defeat it.

As more people learned to read and write, fewer and fewer cultures told stories from memory. The Grimms were educated young men who were trained to find information in books. Unfortunately, no one had thought fairy tales were important enough to write down. The brothers now realized that they needed to go to the source: the storytellers.

"Cinderella" had been told for hundreds of years in many European countries even before French author Charles Perrault wrote down his version. In each country, the story had a different title and the characters had different names. It was Perrault who added the pumpkin carriage, the fairy godmother, and Cinderella's glass slipper to the story. In the German version that the Grimms found, Cinderella does not have a fairy godmother but receives help from a wishing tree that grows on her mother's grave.

The Grimms thought Perrault had done a good job, but they wanted a collection of German tales. They didn't have to go far to find storytellers. Local women seemed to be the best sources for stories. The Grimms' next-door neighbor,

Herr Wild, had four daughters who all loved folktales. The Wilds passed along many of their stories to the brothers. Even the Wilds' nanny and housekeeper, Marie Müller or "Old Marie,"

contributed several stories. One of them was the German version of "Little Red Riding Hood" called "Little Red Cap." Another pair of sisters, Amalie and Jeanette Hassenpflug, knew a dozen stories, including several of the most famous: "Briar Rose," "Tom Thumb," and "Snow White."

Soldiers, farmers, and fishermen also told tales to the brothers. A retired soldier told Jacob several stories in exchange for a pair of pants. The soldier later told Jacob that he thought of him twice a day—whenever he was putting on and taking off his pants.

CHARLES PERRAULT (1628–1703)

JACOB AND WILHELM WERE NOT THE FIRST TO TRY TO PRESERVE FAIRY TALES. A HUNDRED YEARS EARLIER, CHARLES PERRAULT HAD WRITTEN *TALES FROM MOTHER GOOSE.*

CHARLES PERRAULT WAS AN IMPORTANT FRENCH LITERARY FIGURE. HE IS MOST FAMOUS FOR HIS COLLECTION OF FRENCH FAIRY TALES PUBLISHED IN 1697. *TALES FROM MOTHER GOOSE* INCLUDED MANY NOW-FAMOUS STORIES SUCH AS "CINDERELLA," "PUSS IN BOOTS," AND "SLEEPING BEAUTY."

PERRAULT WAS ALSO AN ADVISER TO THE KING OF FRANCE. HE ENCOURAGED LOUIS XIV TO CREATE AESOP'S FOUNTAIN AT VERSAILLES, WHICH INCLUDED THIRTY-NINE STATUES, EACH REPRESENTING ONE OF AESOP'S FABLES.

For six years, the Grimms worked on the fairy tales. It took time to collect the stories and then to organize and edit them. In 1812, Arnim visited the Grimms. When he read their manuscript, he immediately set off to Berlin to find a publisher. Georg Andreas Reimer agreed to make the Grimms' eighty-six stories into a book.

Just five days before Christmas, *Children's and Household Tales* by the Brothers Grimm was published.

Chapter 6
The Search Continues

Children's and Household Tales was an immediate success. The arrival of the fairy tales gave the German people a renewed sense of pride in their country—just as the Grimms had hoped. All nine hundred copies of the book were sold within a few short months. Children read the fairy tales over and over, memorizing their favorites.

Adults loved the book, too, but some thought the fairy tales were too violent. One mother told Wilhelm she refused to let her children read the book because of one story. In it, children are tricked into killing their friends. Wilhelm adamantly defended the story: His own mother had told it to him as a child, and, as a result, he played with his friends more carefully.

Their publisher immediately asked for more fairy tales. Wilhelm began to travel to different towns to meet storytellers. He was amazed how famous the fairy tales had made him and Jacob. Storytellers all across Germany had heard of the brothers and were very willing to tell Wilhelm their stories.

One woman, Dorothea Viehmann, lived in a village on the outskirts of Kassel. Wilhelm was amazed at how clearly and precisely she told stories. Dorothea would tell Wilhelm a story, and then slowly tell it again—

DOROTHEA VIEHMANN

without changing a single word—so he could write it down. Wilhelm also traveled out into the countryside to meet the Haxthausen family. The Haxthausens loved German folklore. They sang old songs, told many folktales, and even wore old-fashioned clothing. Their two daughters, Anna and Ludowine, told Wilhelm twenty of the seventy stories he put in the second volume!

While Wilhelm worked to collect stories for their new book, Jacob began to worry about his job at the library. Napoleon was losing power. King Jerome was scared he would not be the ruler of Kassel for much longer.

King Jerome ordered Jacob to pack up the palace's important books and works of art and ship them to France. This was very upsetting to Jacob. These were valuable works of German art and literature! He couldn't let the French have them! He tried to convince the king that none of it was worth taking, but he didn't succeed. The German treasures were sent to France.

It seemed that the French would never leave Germany. But early one morning in October 1813, wagons and carriages rushed past the Grimms' home. Jacob woke to find the French fleeing town. The Germans were finally free!

A month later, Tante Zimmer, the brothers' favorite aunt, returned to Kassel. Jacob and Wilhelm joined the crowd dancing and celebrating in the street.

A couple of months later, Jacob became

secretary to a German government official. Jacob made two trips to Paris to retrieve the very same books and paintings he had shipped to France.

Wilhelm became the secretary to the librarian in Kassel. Though his job was very boring, he was busy editing the second volume of fairy tales. In the first volume, Wilhelm had kept many of the stories just as they'd been told to him. But for their second book, he made the stories simpler and easier to understand. He even changed many names of the original titles. "Rumpenstunzchen" became "Rumpelstiltskin," and "Little Brother and Sister" became "Hansel and Gretel."

In January 1815, Wilhelm sent the second fairy-tale volume to Jacob, who was now living in Vienna. Jacob did not like that the book was much thinner than the first. He was also upset that Wilhelm had not included all of his footnotes.

A footnote is an extra bit of helpful information included at the bottom of a page in a book. Jacob's notes had been about the history of the fairy tales. But Wilhelm wanted the second volume to be better suited for children, not scholars.

The brothers must have worked through their differences, because later that year, the second collection of seventy fairy tales was published with a few more of Jacob's footnotes included.

Jacob lived in Vienna for almost two years. In April 1815, he received tragic news from Wilhelm. Tante Zimmer, the brothers' aunt, had died. Her death had an enormous impact on the brothers. As soon as he could, Jacob returned home to Kassel. The brothers decided never to live apart again.

Chapter 7
The Best Years

For the next thirteen years, Jacob and Wilhelm worked at the library in Kassel together. These were some of the most productive and happy years of their lives. Wilhelm continued to edit the fairy tales; but both brothers turned to other projects.

In 1816, Wilhelm published two editions of *German Legends*, a collection of stories rooted in history. Neither of them became as popular as the fairy tales.

Jacob began studying the history of the German language. In 1819, he published *German Grammar*. The book traced the development of Germanic languages. This had never been done before. People knew that languages such as French, Spanish, Italian, and Latin were connected to one another. But Jacob proved that German, Greek, and even Sanskrit, a language once spoken in parts of India, were also connected to French and Spanish.

Jacob also discovered that words follow patterns when they change from language to language. This rule is called Grimm's Law. It explained why words such as the English word *mother* and the German word *mutter* were so similar. Many important thinkers consider this to be Jacob's most important contribution to the study of language.

Jacob's boss did not appreciate his work. In fact, when he heard about *German Grammar*, he got angry. He worried that Jacob was neglecting his job in the library to write "extras."

But scholars and historians found Jacob's work very interesting. So did ordinary people. *German Grammar* became a national best seller. In fact, it sold better than the fairy tales! Within a year, Jacob began working on the next edition.

In 1823, a man named Edgar Taylor translated the Grimms' fairy tales into English and called it *German Popular Stories*. For the first time, the stories were illustrated. Taylor had asked a famous British cartoonist, George Cruikshank, to help bring the tales to life. The book sold very well and spread the brothers' fame even further.

EDGAR TAYLOR

GEORGE CRUIKSHANK (1792–1878)

GEORGE CRUIKSHANK WAS A WELL-KNOWN BRITISH ILLUSTRATOR. GEORGE'S FATHER, ISAAC, HAD BEEN FAMOUS FOR HIS CARICATURES. CARICATURES ARE EXAGGERATED, OFTEN COMICAL ILLUSTRATIONS OF PEOPLE. GEORGE LEARNED HOW TO DRAW FROM HIS FATHER. FOR MANY YEARS, HE DREW CARTOONS THAT MADE FUN OF BRITISH POLITICIANS AS WELL AS THE FAMILY OF KING GEORGE IV.

WHEN GEORGE WAS TWENTY-EIGHT YEARS OLD, HE STARTED ILLUSTRATING BOOKS. IN 1824, HE CREATED TWENTY-TWO ILLUSTRATIONS FOR *GERMAN POPULAR STORIES*. GEORGE BECAME EVEN MORE FAMOUS AFTER HE ILLUSTRATED SEVERAL BOOKS WRITTEN BY HIS GOOD FRIEND CHARLES DICKENS. OVER THE COURSE OF HIS LIFE, GEORGE CRUIKSHANK CREATED NEARLY TEN THOUSAND ILLUSTRATIONS AND PRINTS.

The success of the English fairy tales inspired Jacob and Wilhelm to add illustrations to their books. Their brother Ludwig had become a well-known painter in Germany. In 1825, they published a new edition of the tales with pictures by Ludwig.

That same year, Wilhelm married Dorothea Wild. Dorothea's family had contributed many fairy tales when Wilhelm was first collecting them.

For fourteen years, Dorothea and Wilhelm had been close friends. The newlyweds asked Jacob to come and live with them.

A year later, in 1826, Dorothea gave birth to her and Wilhelm's first child. They named him Jacob. But within the year, the baby became ill and died. Wilhelm was heartbroken. Two years later, in 1828, Dorothea had a second son, Herman.

Jacob and Wilhelm loved living and working in Kassel. They took long walks every afternoon and had plenty of time to read and write. But in 1829, they were passed over for better jobs. So the Grimms accepted jobs at the University of Göttingen in the province of Hanover. Jacob was to be a professor, and both he and Wilhelm would work in the library. The brothers' quiet and productive years in Kassel had come to an end.

UNIVERSITY OF GÖTTINGEN

Chapter 8
Folk Heroes

Jacob and Wilhelm were sad to leave Kassel. Dorothea was pregnant and not feeling well. So she and two-year-old Herman stayed behind. It must have been hard for Wilhelm to say good-bye to his wife and baby. However, the brothers arrived at their new home to a warm welcome: A friend had already lit fires in the stoves.

Weeks later, Wilhelm returned for his wife and son. And three months later, Dorothea gave birth to another son, Rudolf.

Sadly, Jacob was not very happy with his new life in Göttingen. He had to prepare lectures, which left little time to read the books he wanted. Jacob was not a very good teacher. He didn't let his students ask questions because he didn't like to be distracted. He wanted to maintain control of the classroom.

Wilhelm proved to be a much better teacher than Jacob. He was patient with his students' mistakes and a very popular lecturer.

Twenty-two students signed up for his first class on medieval German poetry. Jacob had had only eight students when he taught the same poetry class!

But Jacob was receiving more and more praise for his work as a language scholar. The university let Jacob have more time for research.

In 1832, Dorothea gave birth to a baby girl named Auguste. She and Wilhelm now had three healthy children. Jacob was a devoted uncle.

It was a happy time for the brothers until their sister, Lotte, became seriously ill. She died on June 15, 1833.

Lotte's death was particularly hard for Wilhelm. For two years, he found it difficult to write or work. Jacob, however, turned his focus to German mythology.

The most famous myths—stories told to help explain the world around us—are from ancient Greece and Rome. One Greek myth tells how the earth was formed. Another tells why the peacock's feathers look like eyes. Many other myths tell how the Greek and Roman gods interfered in the lives of human beings.

Jacob's work *German Mythology,* published in 1835, completely changed how people thought about the German people and their culture. Many people knew the myths from ancient Greece and

Rome. But very few knew any German myths. Instead, they thought ancient Germans were barbaric. Now, because of Jacob, people could read these ancient stories and see that ancient Germans were actually civilized people with a system of law and faith in the divine. People who study German mythology today refer to the time before 1835 as "before Grimm" and the years after 1835 as "after Grimm."

In 1837, Ernest Augustus became king of Hanover. He did not rule fairly and did not respect his people. He demanded that the university professors were to be loyal to him. He wanted the professors to sign an oath.

ERNEST AUGUSTUS

Jacob and Wilhelm, along with five other professors, refused. Instead, they sent a protest to the king. They did not think a ruler should have the power to take away the people's rights. These seven professors became known as the Göttingen Seven.

Ernest Augustus was furious. The University of Göttingen fired the seven professors, and the king exiled the three leaders, one of whom was Jacob. But many students supported their professors.

They threw rocks in the windows of the professors who had obeyed the king. King Augustus told the students that if they tried to help the seven professors, they would be charged a huge fine. But the students refused to listen.

On December 17, 1837, soldiers escorted three leaders of the Göttingen Seven, including Jacob, to the border of Hanover. They were being forced to leave the province. Nearly three hundred students walked twenty miles in the freezing cold to meet their professors at the border town of Witzenhausen. As a sign of loyalty to their professors and of protest to the king, they unhooked the horses from the professors' carriages. The students themselves pulled the carriages across the bridge and out of the territory of Ernest Augustus.

The news spread across the German provinces. Many people were proud that the professors had stood up to the king. The bridge crossing became known as the Witzenhausen Escort. Like characters in one of their own stories, the Brothers Grimm had become folk heroes.

Chapter 9
Celebrities

After the Witzenhausen Escort, Jacob returned to Kassel. In the fall of 1838, Wilhelm and his family joined Jacob and their younger brother Ludwig in Kassel.

Jacob and Wilhelm had a difficult time finding work. Many people were now scared to hire the men who had rebelled against the king. But Jacob and Wilhelm were not discouraged. All over Germany, students and faculty—even entire towns—collected money for the seven professors. One town

sent the professors 1,600 talers. That was enough money for two people to live on for a year.

Soon, a publisher asked Jacob and Wilhelm to create a German dictionary. The dictionary would explain how words were used from the sixteenth century up to the present day. The publisher wanted every possible German word listed with examples for how to use it in a sentence.

Jacob and Wilhelm knew they couldn't complete the dictionary alone. So they asked more than fifty scholars to help collect words. They sent each scholar strips of paper that were all the same size.

The brothers wanted to have an organized system to keep track of the words. Soon, the Grimms' desks were covered with thousands of little white strips of paper!

At this time, the most important European scholars were all members of the Berlin Academy of Sciences. The Berlin Academy awarded money to scholars for their research projects. Wilhelm and Jacob were invited to join the Academy.

BERLIN ACADEMY OF SCIENCES

They happily accepted, though it meant moving to the bustling city of Berlin. Then in November 1840 came more good news. The new king of Prussia decided to fund Jacob and Wilhelm's work on the German dictionary. They would never have to worry about money again.

A few weeks later, Jacob traveled to Berlin to look for an apartment. He couldn't believe how well-known he was. Everyone wanted to have him over for dinner. Jacob was invited to so many

parties and dinners that he stayed several weeks longer than planned.

By February 1841, the Grimms had moved to Berlin. Until this time, the brothers had lectured to only small numbers of students. But now that they were members of the Academy, several hundred people came to listen to them speak.

The crowd cheered loudly when Jacob and Wilhelm walked out onstage for their first lecture.

Both brothers were taken aback. Jacob had to pause several times when speaking to collect his thoughts. Wilhelm was moved to tears. They had never received such praise for their work!

Jacob and Wilhelm ate dinner with princes. The king invited them to see plays at the palace.

Crowds would gather outside their home and sing songs until Jacob and Wilhelm stepped out onto the balcony. The Grimms were greeted with cheers, speeches, and even gifts.

Jacob and Wilhelm were honored for their work all across the world. Jacob received Prussia's highest award. Before Jacob, only soldiers had been given this honor. France awarded Jacob with the Cross of the Legion of Honor. England made the brothers members of the Philological Society, the oldest society in Great Britain dedicated to studying language. And the United States admitted Jacob into the Academy of the Arts and Sciences. Like the Berlin Academy, it was a group of famous writers, scientists, and teachers.

Important men from all over Europe traveled to Berlin just to meet the famous Brothers Grimm. Neither Jacob nor Wilhelm liked being interrupted from work, but they were kind to their visitors, inviting them in for tea or for a walk in the garden.

One day, Hans Christian Andersen, a famous Danish author, visited the Grimms. In those days, it was polite to bring a letter of introduction when meeting someone for the first time. But Hans Christian Andersen did not think he needed one. Surely, the Grimms had heard of him—he was a famous author of stories for children!

But Andersen was mistaken. Jacob had no idea who he was, and Wilhelm was not home at the time. Andersen was embarrassed to have just shown up on the doorstep of the famous Grimm brothers!

HANS CHRISTIAN ANDERSEN
(1805–1875)

DANISH AUTHOR AND POET HANS CHRISTIAN ANDERSEN WROTE MANY POEMS, PLAYS, AND NOVELS. BUT HE IS BEST KNOWN FOR HIS FAIRY TALES. INSTEAD OF COLLECTING FAIRY TALES, AS THE GRIMMS DID, ANDERSEN MADE UP HIS OWN.

IT IS NOT EASY TO WRITE AN ORIGINAL FAIRY TALE. HANS CHRISTIAN ANDERSEN, HOWEVER, CREATED MANY NEW FAIRY TALES THAT BECAME JUST AS FAMOUS AS THE ONES THAT HAD EXISTED FOR HUNDREDS OF YEARS. HE WROTE "THE LITTLE MERMAID," "THE UGLY DUCKLING," "THE PRINCESS AND THE PEA," "THE EMPEROR'S NEW CLOTHES," AND MANY MORE.

TODAY, THE QUEEN OF DENMARK SPONSORS THE HANS CHRISTIAN ANDERSEN AWARD, WHICH IS GIVEN TO AUTHORS AND ILLUSTRATORS WHO HAVE MADE LASTING CONTRIBUTIONS TO CHILDREN'S LITERATURE.

Chapter 10
Happily Ever After

The Grimms continued to work on their dictionary but made very little progress. It was such a huge job! Jacob concentrated on words beginning with *A* through *C*, while Wilhelm worked only on the letter *D*.

Work on the dictionary wasn't as much fun as collecting fairy tales had been years earlier. Jacob was becoming frustrated with Wilhelm. Wilhelm wasn't as precise with his work as Jacob was, and he often borrowed books from Jacob's study without returning them. Even when Wilhelm did return the books, Jacob complained that Wilhelm was making too much noise by constantly opening and shutting doors.

Finally, in 1854, sixteen years after starting the dictionary, Jacob and Wilhelm published the first volume, *A–Biermolke*. They hadn't even gotten through all the words starting with *B*! The brothers realized that they would never finish the dictionary in their lifetimes.

THE GERMAN DICTIONARY

JACOB AND WILHELM GRIMM BEGAN THE FIRST MAJOR GERMAN DICTIONARY. THEIR GOAL WAS TO GIVE THE HISTORY AND MEANING OF EVERY WORD USED IN GERMAN LITERATURE FROM 1500 TO 1832. THE BROTHERS COMPLETED FOUR VOLUMES. JACOB COMPILED VOLUMES I, III, AND IV, AND WILHELM WROTE VOLUME II. THEIR DICTIONARY WENT UP TO THE WORD *FRUCT*, OR "FRUIT."

AFTER THE BROTHERS DIED, OTHER GERMAN SCHOLARS WORKED TO FINISH IT. IT WASN'T UNTIL 1960—OVER ONE HUNDRED YEARS AFTER THE GRIMMS HAD STARTED—THAT THE DICTIONARY WAS COMPLETED. THEIR DICTIONARY INSPIRED ENGLAND, FRANCE, THE NETHERLANDS, SWEDEN, AND SWITZERLAND TO CREATE DICTIONARIES OF THEIR OWN.

In 1859, Wilhelm and his family took a vacation to the Elbe River. While on the trip, Wilhelm became sick. When he returned home, his health did not improve.

When Wilhelm's fever grew worse, Dorothea and Jacob were worried this would be the end. Jacob stayed by his brother's bedside all night long and through the next day. At times, the fever made Wilhelm think that Jacob was not his brother but a painting! At other times, Wilhelm was clearheaded.

Just two hours before he died, Wilhelm told one of his favorite stories. Then at three o'clock in the afternoon on December 16, 1859, Wilhelm died.

His body was laid in his study. Jacob kept coming to the room to look at the brother and best friend he would never see again. For a while, all of Wilhelm's books and papers were kept just as he had left them so that a painter could record Wilhelm's study.

Would Jacob be able to go on without his beloved Wilhelm? They were famous as the Brothers Grimm, after all. Berlin newspapers reported that when Jacob was alone in the house, he spent his time looking for Wilhelm. But this was not true. Jacob continued to live and work just as he had before Wilhelm's death.

Jacob finished Wilhelm's last project for him. Jacob also sent the publisher the second piece of the dictionary, which Wilhelm had finished.

It went up to the letter *D*. Jacob then set to work on the next two volumes of the dictionary.

In the fall, Jacob took a trip to the mountains.

The fresh air and travel seemed at first to be good for him. But when he returned home, he caught a cold, which soon developed into a more serious illness.

One Saturday afternoon in September, Jacob was sitting with his niece, Auguste, when he suffered a stroke. Jacob's right arm couldn't move, and he could no longer speak. The next day, Jacob's heart beat so wildly, Auguste thought it might explode. At one point, Jacob looked steadily at a photograph of Wilhelm. And then, just after ten o'clock in the evening on September 20, 1863, Jacob died.

Many people attended Jacob's funeral. Journals and newspapers published articles about his life.

In later years, people would argue over which of the brothers was the greater scholar. However, today, we remember Jacob and Wilhelm Grimm most for their fairy tales. The fairy tales live on because they teach us to see the world differently. There are dragons and witches and difficult times, but there are also beautiful princesses and brave princes, daring quests, and happily-ever-afters.

Next to the Bible, *Children's and Household Tales* is still the most widely read book in Germany. But Jacob and Wilhelm didn't just preserve these fairy tales for the German people—they did so for the world. Grimms' fairy tales have been translated into more than 160 different languages and have been illustrated by hundreds of artists. They have also been adapted into countless movies, plays, and television shows.

Wilhelm Grimm once wrote, "In the fairy tales a world of magic is opened up before us, one which still exists among us in secret forests, in underground caves, and in the deepest sea, and it is still visible to children." The work of the Brothers Grimm certainly has earned its place in the hearts—and on the bookshelves—of children around the world.

TIMELINE OF THE BROTHERS GRIMM'S LIVES

1785	Jacob is born on January 4
1786	Wilhelm is born on February 24
1791	The Grimm family moves to Steinau
1796	Philipp Grimm, their father, dies
1798	The brothers go away to school in Kassel
1802	Jacob goes to university at Marburg
1803	Wilhelm joins Jacob at university
1804	Jacob is Savigny's assistant in Paris
1806	The brothers begin collecting fairy tales
1808	Dorothea Grimm, their mother, dies Jacob becomes librarian to King Jerome Bonaparte
1812	Publish Volume I of *Children's and Household Tales*
1815	Publish Volume II of *Children's and Household Tales*
1816-1818	Wilhelm publishes two volumes of *German Legends*
1819	Jacob finishes *German Grammar*
1825	Publish a version of the fairy tales illustrated by Ludwig Wilhelm marries Henriette Dorothea Wild
1830	The brothers become professors at the University of Göttingen
1837	Participate in the Göttingen Seven protest
1841	The brothers move to Berlin
1854	Volume I of *German Dictionary* is published
1859	Wilhelm dies on December 16
1863	Jacob dies on September 20

TIMELINE OF THE WORLD

Thomas Jefferson writes the Declaration of Independence	1776
Astronomer William Herschel discovers the planet Uranus	1781
First hot-air balloon flight across the English Channel	1785
George Washington is inaugurated as the first US president The French Revolution begins	1789
The steamboat is invented by John Fitch	1791
French King Louis XVI is executed	1793
The Republic of Switzerland is formed	1798
A Philadelphia shoemaker designs the first shoes to fit the left and right feet	1800
Meriwether Lewis and William Clark begin their expedition	1804
The Holy Roman Empire is dissolved	1806
Napoleon is defeated at the Battle of Waterloo European leaders meet at the Congress of Vienna	1815
Construction of the Erie Canal begins	1817
John Deere makes the first steel plough	1833
The Alamo, a fort in Texas, is besieged for thirteen days	1836
Inventor Samuel Morse patents his telegraph	1840
Charlotte Brontë's book *Jane Eyre* is published in London	1847
Otto von Bismarck unifies Germany	1871

BIBLIOGRAPHY

* Grimm, Jacob, and Wilhelm Grimm. **Grimm's Complete Fairy Tales**. New York: Barnes & Noble, 1993.

Hettinga, Donald R. **The Brothers Grimm: Two Lives, One Legacy**. New York: Clarion, 2001.

* Miller, Raymond H. **The Brothers Grimm**. Farmington Hills, MI: KidHaven, 2006.

Peppard, Murray B. **Paths through the Forest: A Biography of the Brothers Grimm**. New York: Holt, Rinehart and Winston, 1971.

* Zipes, Jack. **The Brothers Grimm: From Enchanted Forests to the Modern World**. New York: Palgrave MacMillan, 2002.

* Books for young readers

THE TIME-TRAVELING ADVENTURES OF THE ROBBINS TWINS

THE TREASURE CHEST

"Kids who have outgrown the 'Magic Treehouse' may enjoy this new series."
—*School Library Journal*

Join Felix and Maisie Robbins on their trips through time as they meet thrilling historical figures as children in *New York Times* Best-Selling author Ann Hood's *The Treasure Chest*!

Clara Barton

Alexander Hamilton

Pearl Buck

Harry Houdini

Crazy Horse

Queen Liliuokalani

Alexander Graham Bell

Amelia Earhart

Leonardo da Vinci

Anastasia Romanov

www.treasurechestseries.com